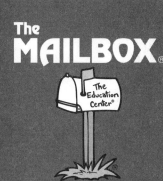

The MAILBOX®

The Education Center®

Phonological & Phonics

M000112008

THE BEST OF TEACHER'S HELPER® Magazine

Kindergarten

The best reproducible activities from the 2005–2008 issues of *Teacher's Helper*® magazine

- **Rhyming**
- **Beginning sounds**
- **Ending sounds**
- **Initial consonants**
- **Final consonants**
- **Word families**
- **CVC words**
- **Digraphs**

Managing Editor: Lynn Drolet

Editorial Team: Becky S. Andrews, Diane Badden, Kimberley Bruck, Karen A. Brudnak, Pam Crane, Georgia Davis, Lynette Dickerson, Tazmen Hansen, Marsha Heim, Lori Z. Henry, Debra Liverman, Kitty Lowrance, Dorothy C. McKinney, Thad H. McLaurin, Sharon Murphy, Jennifer Nunn, Mark Rainey, Hope Rodgers, Rebecca Saunders, Rachael Traylor, Zane Williard

Reinforce and assess key literacy skills!

www.themailbox.com

©2009 The Mailbox® Books
All rights reserved.
ISBN10 #1-56234-911-2 • ISBN13 #978-1-56234-911-0

Printed in the United States
10 9 8 7 6 5 4 3 2 1

Table of

Contents

Soooo many skills!

Name _____

Dog and Cat

🖍 Color the rhyming pictures.

The Best of Teacher's Helper® Phonological Awareness & Phonics • ©The Mailbox® Books • TEC61238 • Key p. 115

Name

Fox and Bear

Color the rhyming pictures.

Name _____

Hen and Goat

✂ Cut.

🖊 Glue to match the rhyming pictures.

10

The Best of Teacher's Helper® Phonological Awareness & Phonics • ©The Mailbox® Books • TEC61238 • Key p. 115

Name

Snake and Pig

✂ Cut.

🍼 Glue to match the rhyming pictures.

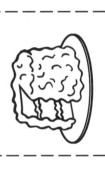

The Best of Teacher's Helper® Phonological Awareness & Phonics • ©The Mailbox® Books • TEC61238 • Key p. 115

7

∞ Name _____

Bug and Bee

Cut. Glue to match the rhyming pictures.

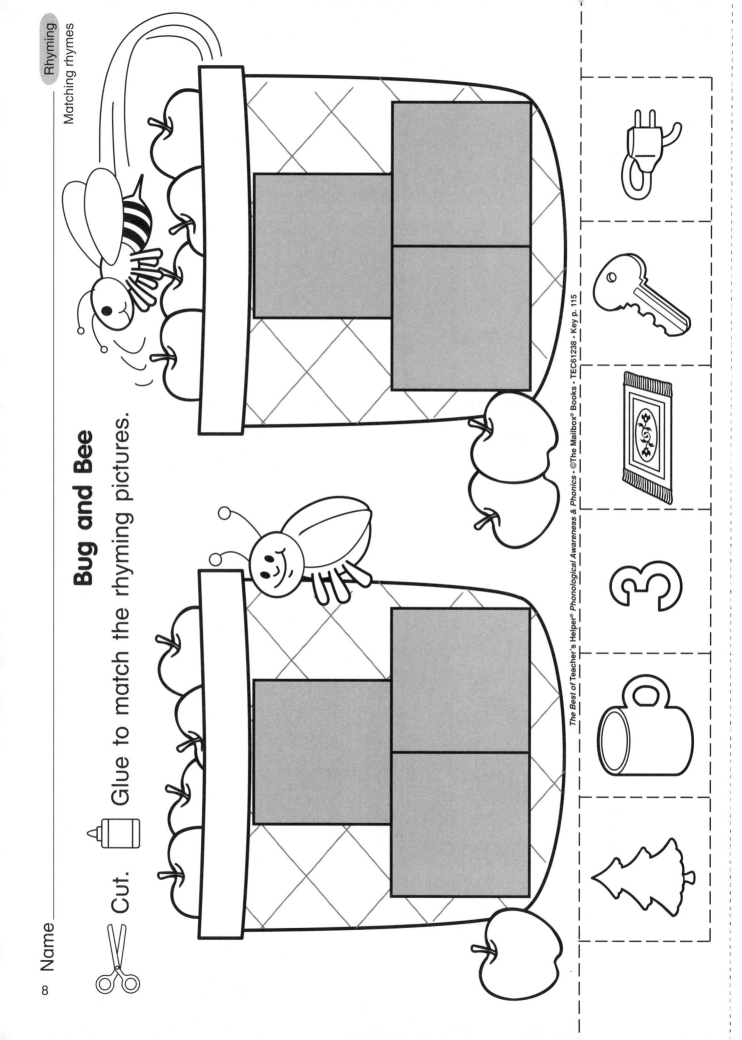

Cake and Bun

Color the rhyming pictures.

Name_____

Bread and Jam

 Color the rhyming pictures.

The Best of Teacher's Helper® Phonological Awareness & Phonics •©The Mailbox® Books • TEC61238 • Key p. 115

Name _____

Pear and Pie

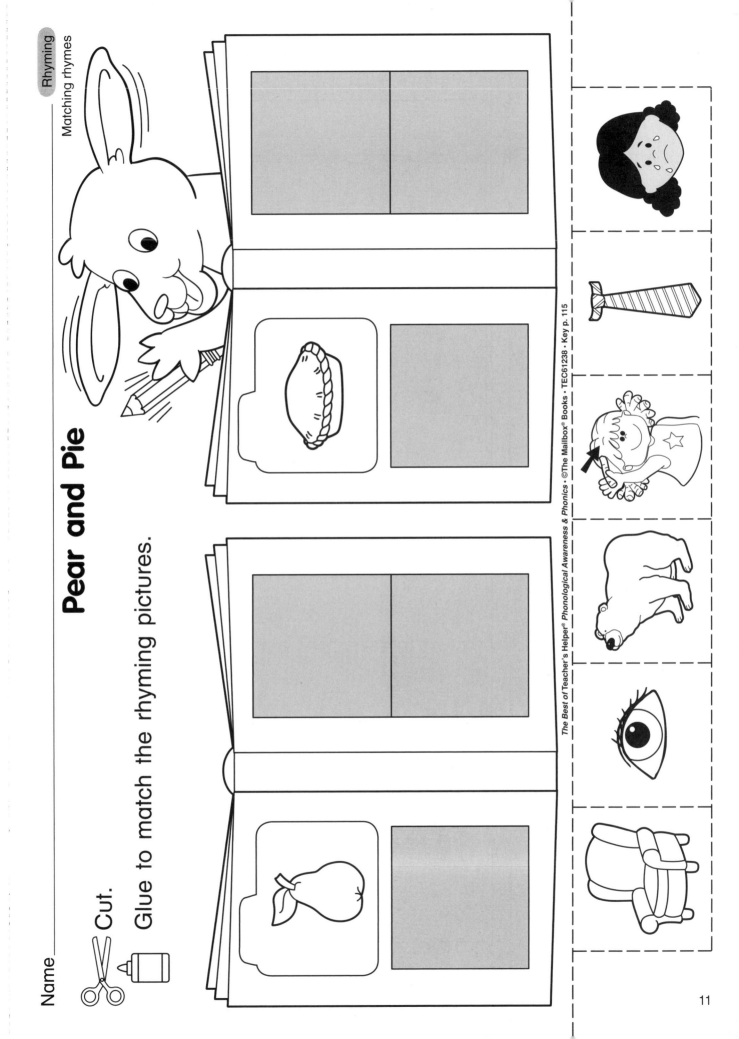

Cut.

Glue to match the rhyming pictures.

The Best of Teacher's Helper® Phonological Awareness & Phonics · ©The Mailbox® Books · TEC61238 · Key p. 115

11

Name

12

Corn and Chip

Cut.

Glue to match the rhyming pictures.

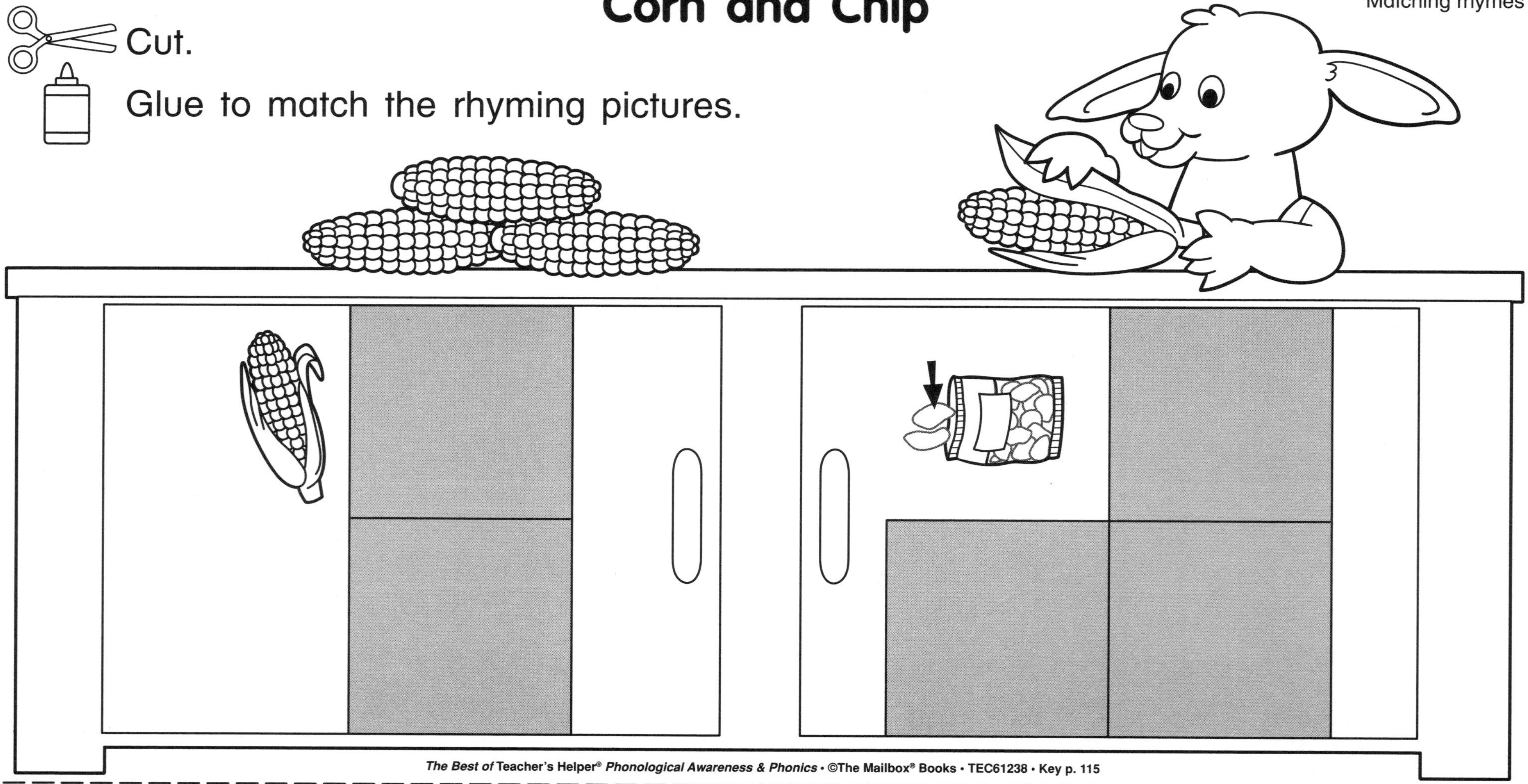

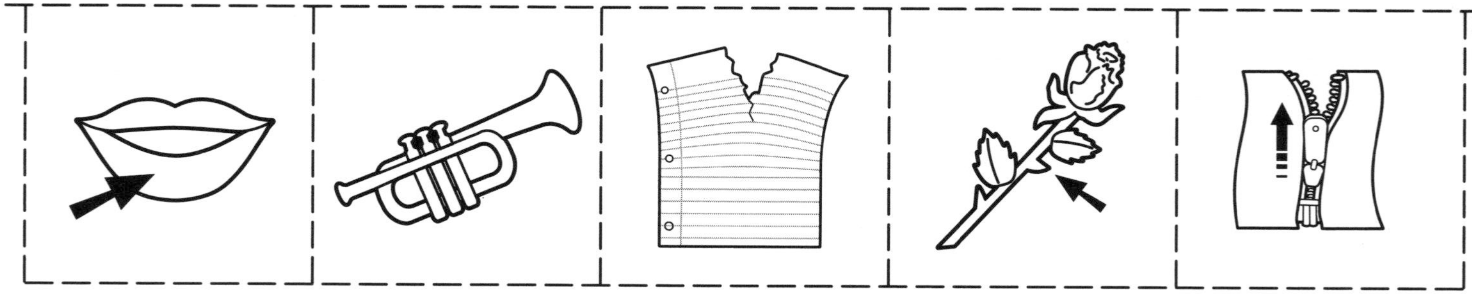

Name _____

A Mouse and His House

 Cut. Glue to match the rhyming pictures.

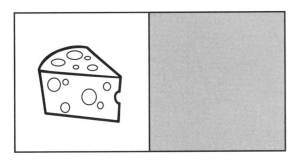

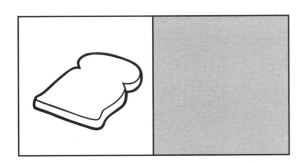

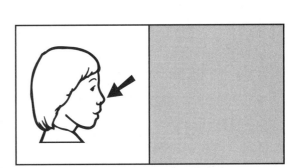

Name _____

Apple Treat

 Color.  Cut.

Glue to match the rhyming pictures.

The Best of Teacher's Helper® *Phonological Awareness & Phonics* • ©The Mailbox® Books • TEC61238 • Key p. 115

Name _____

Up the Ladder!

 Color.  Cut.

Glue to match the rhyming pictures.

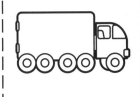

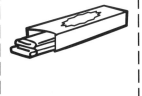

Easy Picking

 Color. ✂ Cut.

Glue to match the rhyming pictures.

5

Load Them Up!

 Color. Cut.

Glue to match the rhyming pictures.

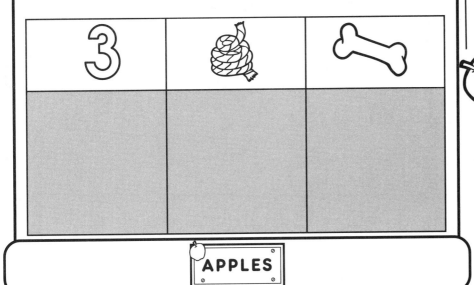

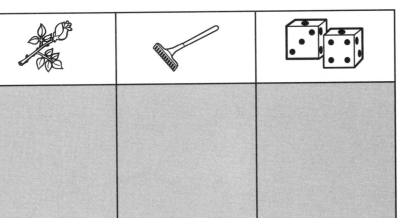

APPLES

Name _____

Mouse's Menu

Color the pictures that begin like  .

The Best of Teacher's Helper® Phonological Awareness & Phonics • ©The Mailbox® Books • TEC61238 • Key p. 116

Name _____

Duck Days

Cut.
Glue the pictures that begin like _____ .

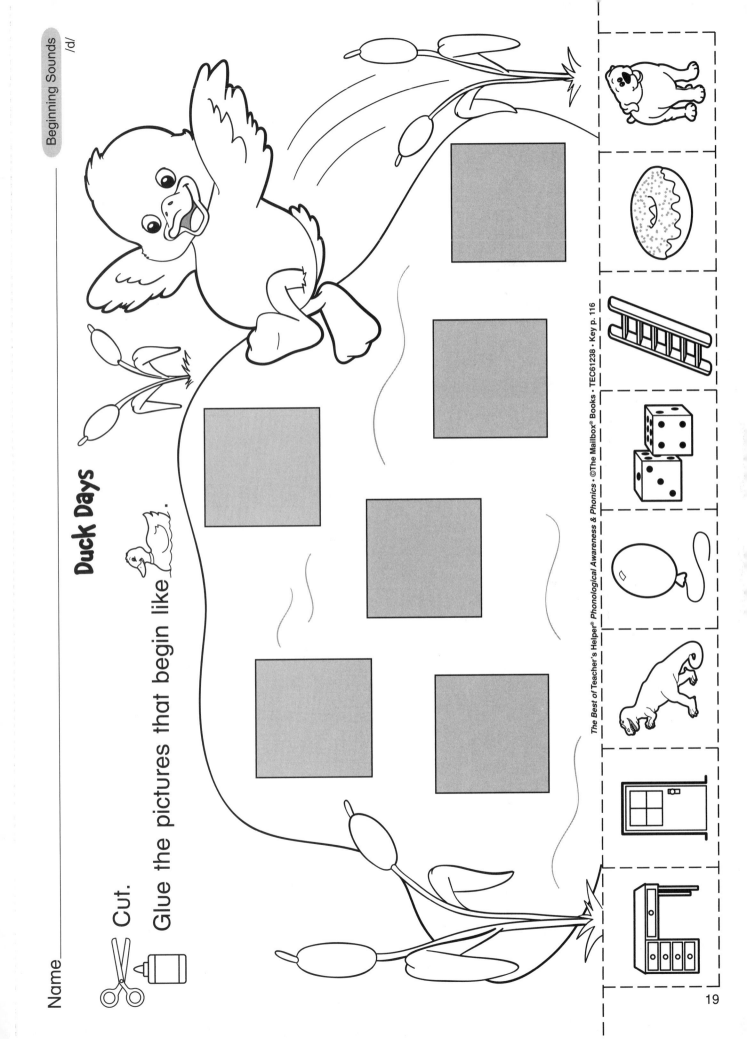

The Best of Teacher's Helper® Phonological Awareness & Phonics • ©The Mailbox® Books • TEC61238 • Key p. 116

19

Name _____

Naughty Goat

Color the pictures that begin like .

Name _____

Horse's Hay

✂ Cut.

Glue the pictures that begin like 🐴.

The Best of Teacher's Helper® Phonological Awareness & Phonics · ©The Mailbox® Books · TEC61238 · Key p. 116

21

Name _____

Cows' Pasture

Color the pictures that begin like .

The Best of Teacher's Helper® Phonological Awareness & Phonics • ©The Mailbox® Books • TEC61238 • Key p. 117

Name _____

Farmer Mouse

 Cut.

Glue the pictures that begin like .

The Best of Teacher's Helper® Phonological Awareness & Phonics • ©The Mailbox® Books • TEC61238 • Key p. 117

Name _____

Pigging Out!

 Cut.

Glue the pictures that begin like .

The Best of Teacher's Helper® Phonological Awareness & Phonics • ©The Mailbox® Books • TEC61238 • Key p. 117

24

Wake Up, Rooster!

Color the pictures that begin like

Name _____

Lovely Leaves

✂ Cut.

🍶 Glue the pictures that begin like 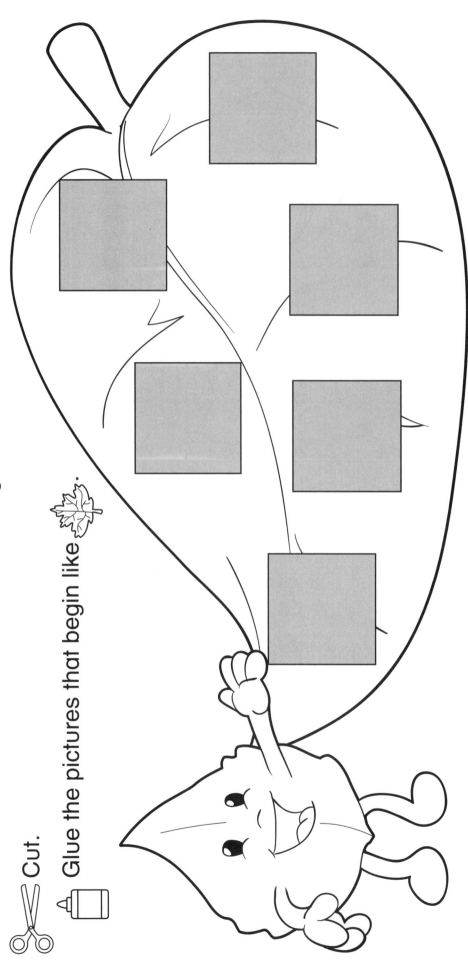 🍁 .

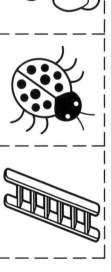

The Best of Teacher's Helper® Phonological Awareness & Phonics · ©The Mailbox® Books · TEC61238 · Key p. 117

Name_____

Time to Rake

Color.

Cut.

Glue the pictures that begin like 🎈.

Almost Done!

 Color.

 Cut.

Glue the pictures that begin like  .

The Best of Teacher's Helper® Phonological Awareness & Phonics • ©The Mailbox® Books • TEC61238 • Key p. 117

Huff and Puff

Color.

Cut.

Glue the pictures that begin like .

Name_____

Windy Day

Color.

Cut.

Glue the pictures that begin like 🌙 .

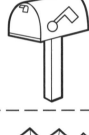

The Best of Teacher's Helper® *Phonological Awareness & Phonics* •©The Mailbox® Books • TEC61238 • Key p. 118

Name_____

Stack of Bags

Color.

Cut.

Glue the pictures that begin like 🧹.

Peek Out!

Color.

Cut.

Glue the pictures that begin like 🦭.

The Best of Teacher's Helper® *Phonological Awareness & Phonics* • ©The Mailbox® Books • TEC61238 • Key p. 118

Name_____

Pile 'em Up!

Color.

Cut.

Glue the pictures that begin like 🪥.

Name_____

Touchdown!

 Color.

 Cut. Glue to match the beginning sounds.

The Best of Teacher's Helper® Phonological Awareness & Phonics • ©The Mailbox® Books • TEC61238 • Key p. 118

34

 Cut.

Ready to Go!

Glue to match the ending sounds.

    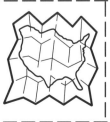 

Balloon Buddies

 Cut.

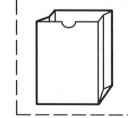 Glue to match the ending sounds.

Name_____

 Cut.

Into the Clouds

Glue to match the ending sounds.

The Best of Teacher's Helper® Phonological Awareness & Phonics • ©The Mailbox® Books • TEC61238 • Key p. 119

Name _____

Looking Down

🖍 Color by the code.

Color Code

— red

— yellow

The Best of Teacher's Helper® *Phonological Awareness & Phonics* • ©The Mailbox® Books • TEC61238 • Key p. 119

Name _____

Balloon Festival

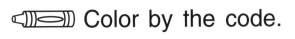 Color by the code.

Color Code

 — blue

— orange

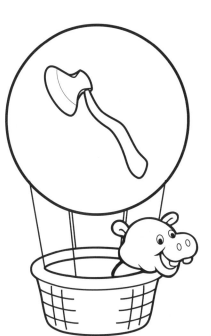

Name _____

40

Happy Landings

Do the words end with the same sound?

Circle.

yes no

yes no

yes no

yes no

yes no

yes no

yes no

Name_____

Dixie Duck

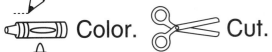 Trace.

Color. 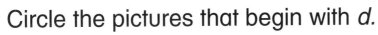 Cut.

Glue the pictures that begin with *d.*

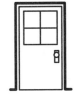

Circle the pictures that begin with *d.*

Name_____

Flappy Fish

 Trace.

 Color.  Cut.

 Glue the pictures that begin with *f*.

f

F f

 Circle the pictures that begin with *f*.

  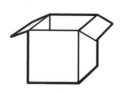  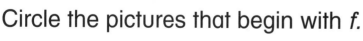

42   *The Best of Teacher's Helper® Phonological Awareness & Phonics • ©The Mailbox® Books • TEC61238 • Key p. 119*

Name_____

g

Gruffy Goat

Trace.

Color. Cut.

Glue the pictures that begin with *g*.

Circle the pictures that begin with *g*.

GAS

Name_____

Harry Horse

 Trace.

 Color. 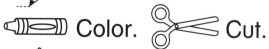 Cut.

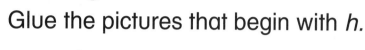 Glue the pictures that begin with *h*.

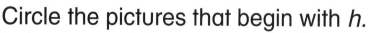

 Circle the pictures that begin with *h*.

44

Name_____

Kalen Kitten

Trace.

Color.   Cut.

Glue the pictures that begin with *k*.

k

K k

Circle the pictures that begin with *k*.

Name_____

Reggie Rabbit

  Trace.

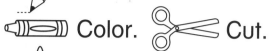 Color. Cut.

Glue the pictures that begin with *r*.

 Circle the pictures that begin with *r*.

Name_____

Sandy Seal

 Trace.

 Color.  Cut.

 Glue the pictures that begin with *s*.

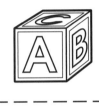

 Circle the pictures that begin with *s*.

The Best of Teacher's Helper® Phonological Awareness & Phonics • ©The Mailbox® Books • TEC61238 • Key p. 120

Name _____

48

At the Fair

Color the pictures with the matching beginning sounds.

Tickets

Gate

The Best of Teacher's Helper® *Phonological Awareness & Phonics* • ©The Mailbox® Books • TEC61238 • Key p. 120

Name _____

Fun and Games!

✂ Cut.

🧴 Glue to match the beginning sounds.

Ball Throw

Ring Toss

The Best of Teacher's Helper® Phonological Awareness & Phonics · ©The Mailbox® Books · TEC61238 · Key p. 120

Name

50

So Much Food!

Color the pictures with the matching beginning sounds.

Cotton Candy

Hot Dogs

Name _____

Showtime!

 Cut.

 Glue to match the beginning sounds.

 **D**ancer

 **S**inger

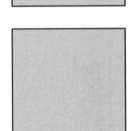

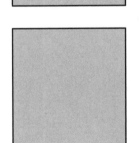

The Best of Teacher's Helper® *Phonological Awareness & Phonics* • ©The Mailbox® Books • TEC61238 • Key p. 120

Name _____

Blue Ribbons!

Color the pictures with the matching beginning sounds.

Jam

Pies

The Best of Teacher's Helper® Phonological Awareness & Phonics • ©The Mailbox® Books • TEC61238 • Key p. 120

Name_____

Top Hat Tricks

 Cut.

Match.

Glue.

Bb	Nn	Tt

Name _____

Initial Consonants

c, g, w

Wave Your Wand

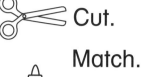 Cut.

Match.

 Glue.

Ww **Cc** **Gg**

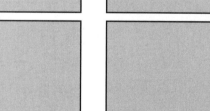

The Best of Teacher's Helper® Phonological Awareness & Phonics • ©The Mailbox® Books • TEC61238 • Key p. 121

Magic Mistake

 Cut.

Match.

 Glue.

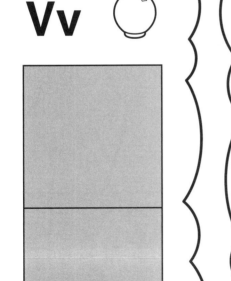

Dd

Vv

Rr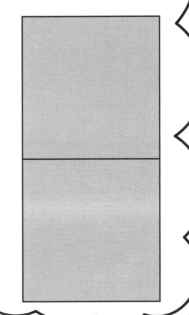

Be Mine

Name_____

Hocus Pocus

 Cut.

Match.

 Glue.

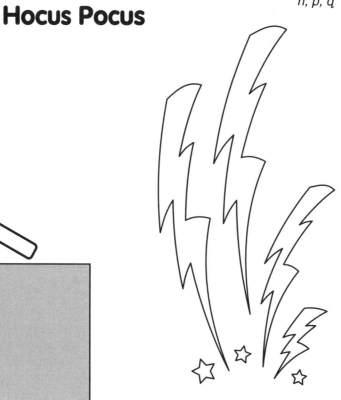

Hh

Pp

Qq

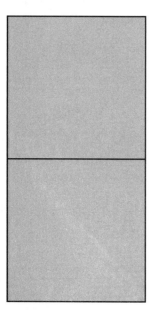

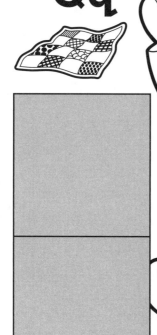

Name_____

Card Tricks

✂ Cut.

🩹 Match.

🧴 Glue.

Ff

Kk

Ll

Name_____

Poof!

✂ Cut.

Match.

🔖 Glue.

Jj

Mm

Ss

j, m, s

Name

Tickets to Ride

Color by the code.

Tickets

Color Code

s as in — blue

m as in — orange

Name _____

60

🖍 Color by the code.

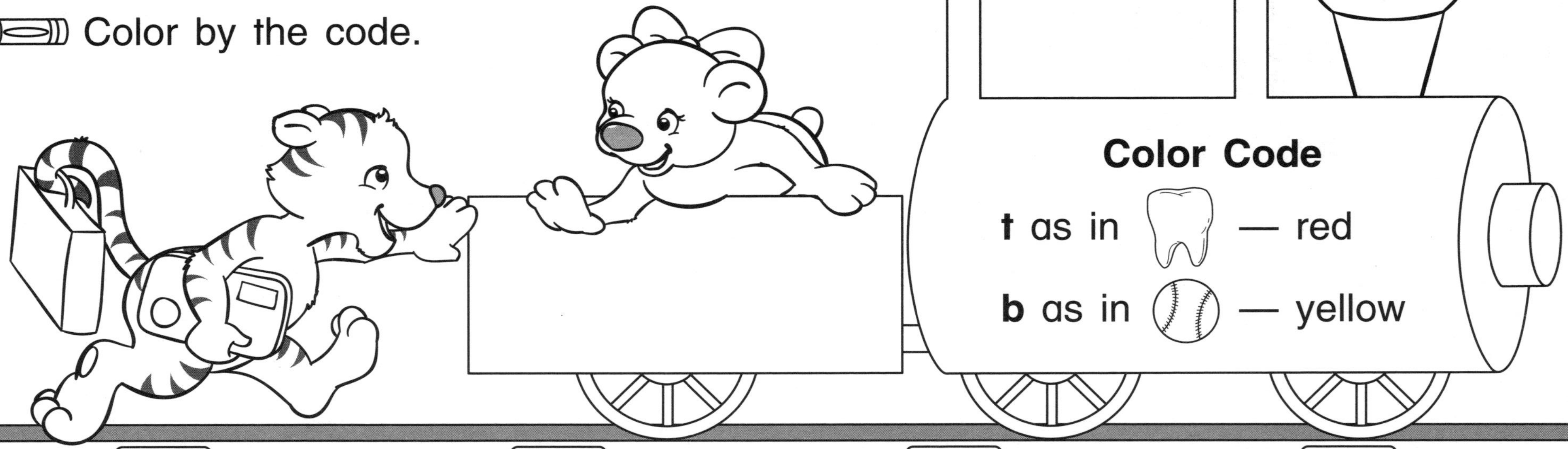

Loading Zone

Color Code

t as in 🦷 — red

b as in ⚾ — yellow

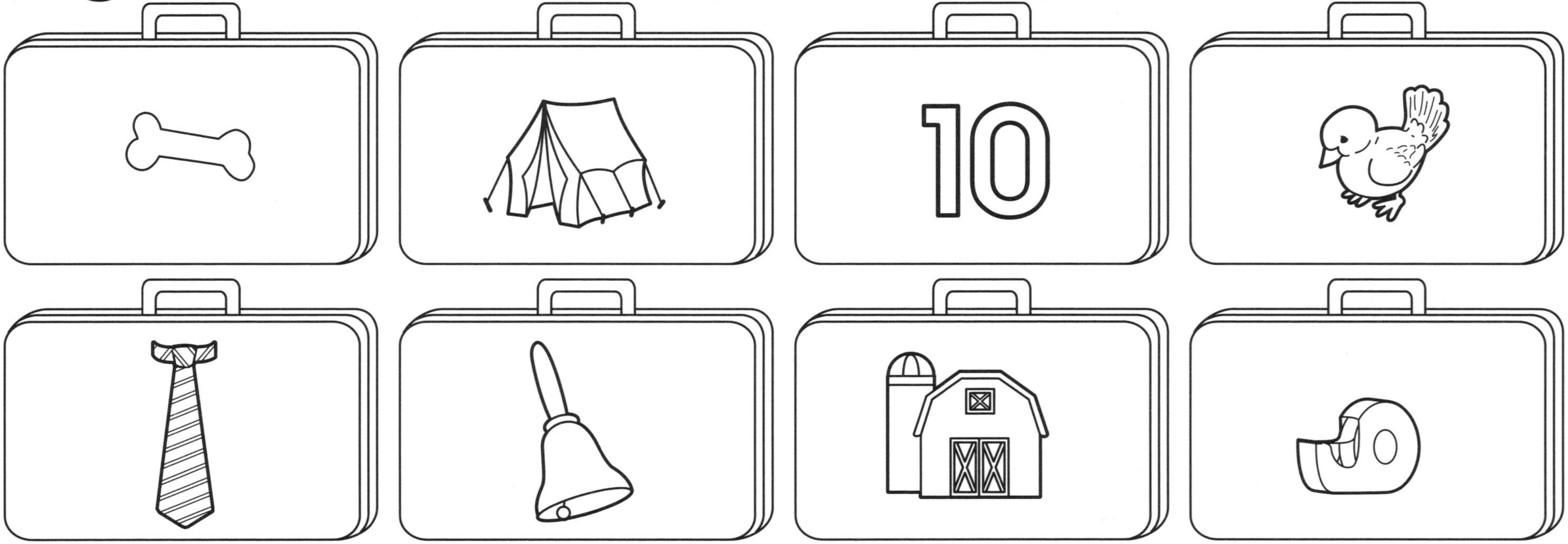

Name _____

Calling All Engines!

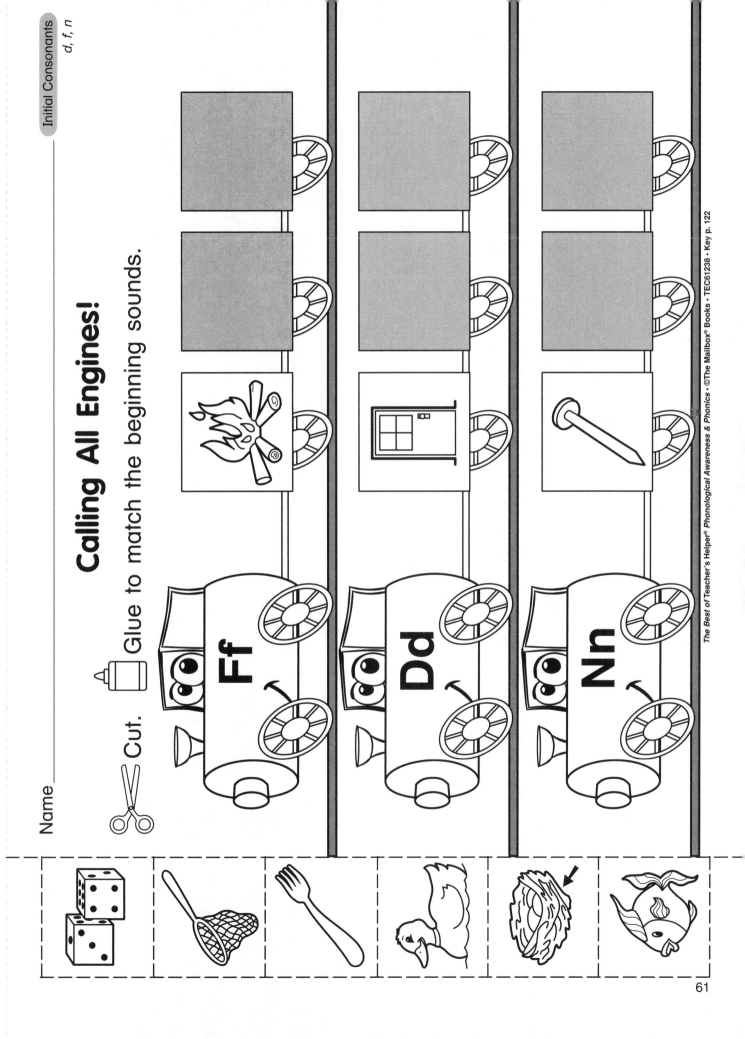

✂ Cut.   🧴 Glue to match the beginning sounds.

Ff

Dd

Nn

The Best of Teacher's Helper® *Phonological Awareness & Phonics* • ©The Mailbox® Books • TEC61238 • Key p. 122

Name

62

Chugging Along

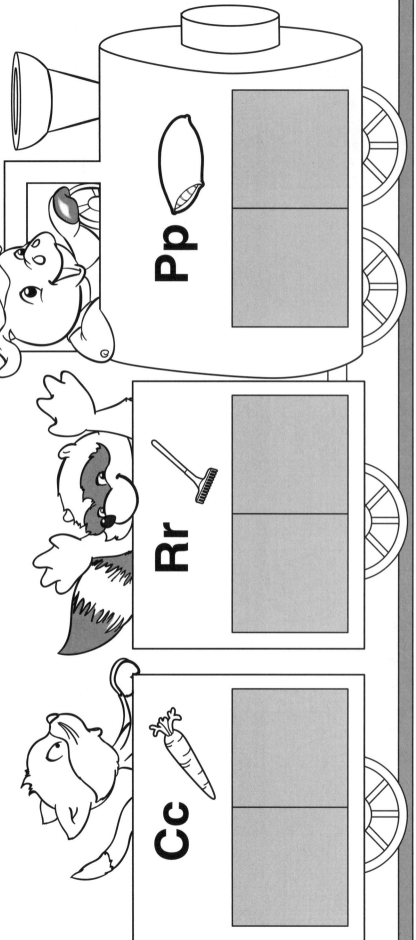

✂ Cut.   🧴 Glue to match the beginning sounds.

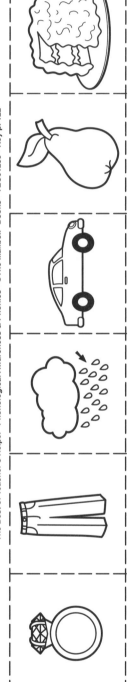

The Best of Teacher's Helper® Phonological Awareness & Phonics • ©The Mailbox® Books • TEC61238 • Key p. 122

Name

Tunnel Time

Cut. Glue to match the beginning sounds.

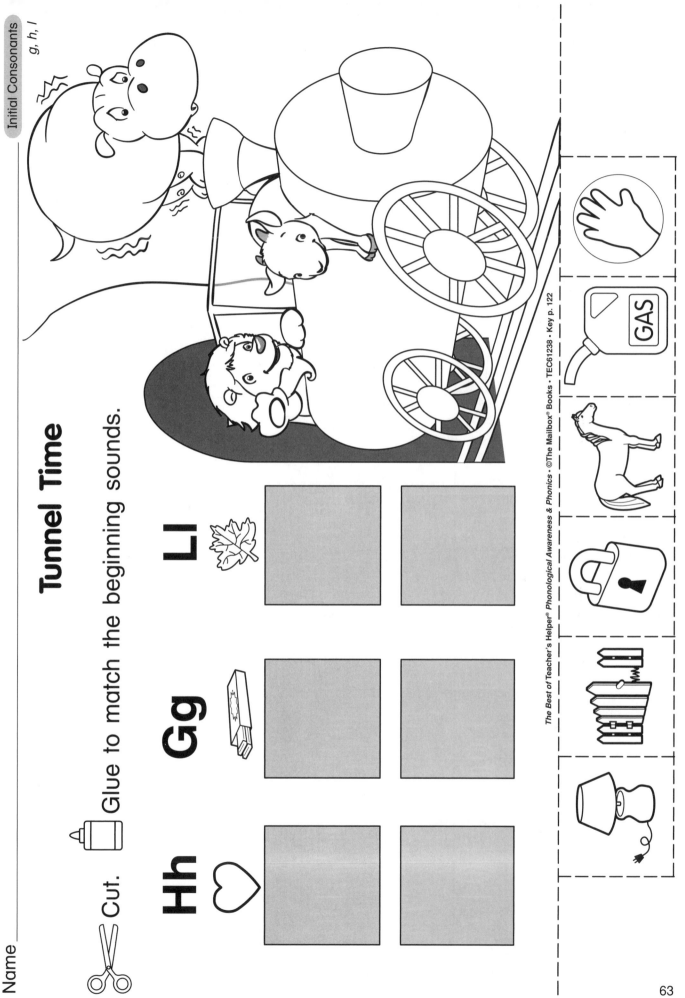

Hh

Gg

Ll

The Best of Teacher's Helper® *Phonological Awareness & Phonics* • ©The Mailbox® Books • TEC61238 • Key p. 122

GAS

63

Full Steam Ahead!

 Write the beginning letter.

Cross out each letter after it has been used.

b c d f g h l m n p r s t

The Best of Teacher's Helper® Phonological Awareness & Phonics • ©The Mailbox® Books • TEC61238 • Key p. 122

Name_____

Among the Stars

Color by the code.

Color Code

b as in 🦋 —yellow

m as in 🌙 —orange

Name_____

Ready for Takeoff!

 Cut. Glue to match the beginning letters.

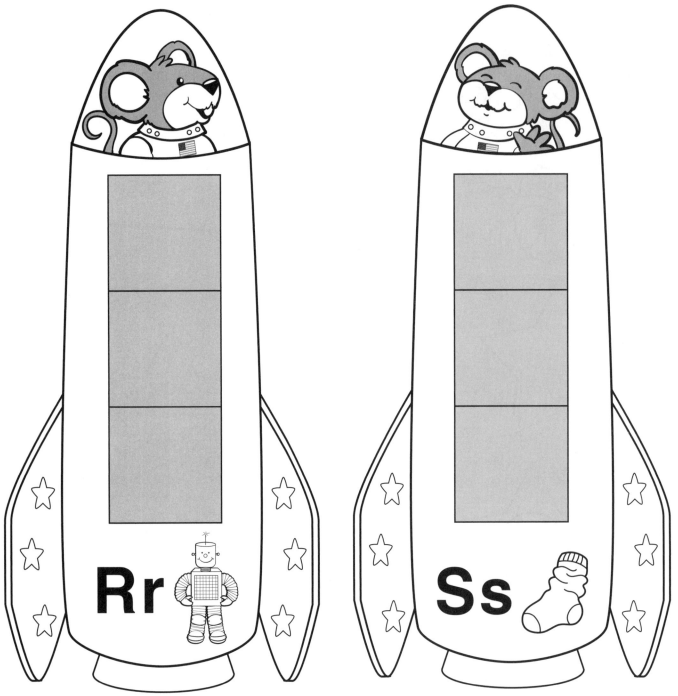

Rr

Ss

Name _____

Space Race

✏ Color the pictures with the matching beginning letters.

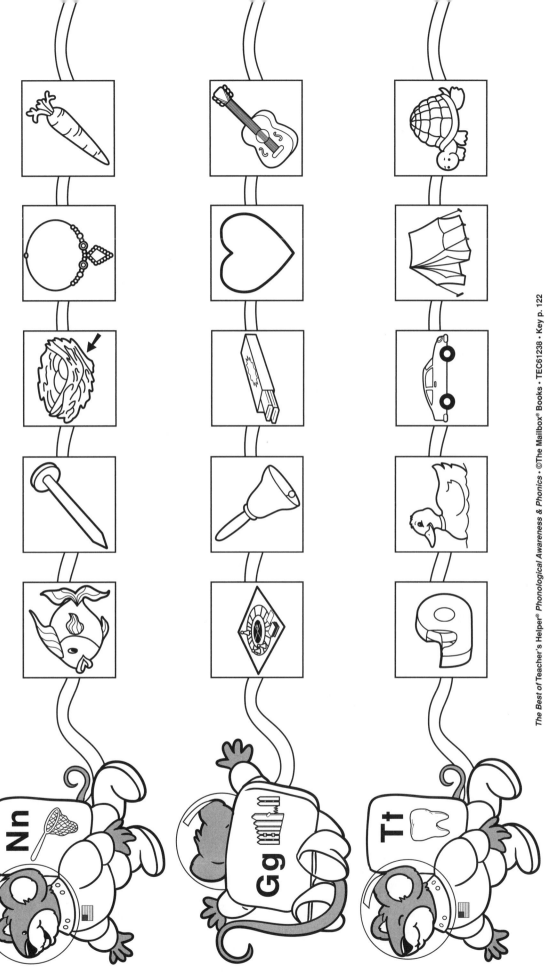

The Best of Teacher's Helper® Phonological Awareness & Phonics • ©The Mailbox® Books • TEC61238 • Key p. 122

Name _____

Moon Mouse

✂ Cut. 🖊 Glue to match the beginning letters.

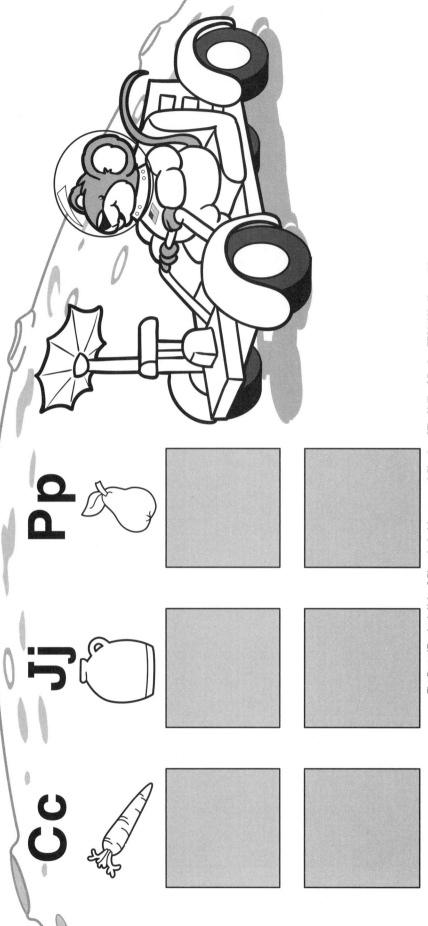

Cc   Jj   Pp

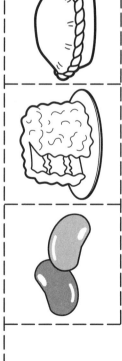

The Best of Teacher's Helper® Phonological Awareness & Phonics • ©The Mailbox® Books • TEC61238 • Key p. 123

Name_____

Soaring Through Space

✏ Write the beginning letter.

l w z

Name_____

A Giant Leap

Write the beginning letter.

Cross out each letter after it has been used.

b c g j l m n
p r s t w z

The Best of Teacher's Helper® Phonological Awareness & Phonics • ©The Mailbox® Books • TEC61238 • Key p. 123

Name _____

Keep On Trucking!

 Cut. Glue to match the beginning sounds.

 Write the beginning letter.

Name _____

Sky Signs

🖍 Color by the code.

✏️ Write the beginning letter.

Color Code

d as in 🐻 —green   h as in ❤️ —red

The Best of Teacher's Helper® Phonological Awareness & Phonics · ©The Mailbox® Books · TEC61238 · Key p. 123

Name_____

Bus Stop

Color by the code.

Write the beginning letter.

Color Code

m as in 🌙 —yellow

p as in 🐷 —blue

74   Name _____

All Aboard!

Color by the code.

Write the beginning letter.

Color Code

c as in ————orange

g as in ————purple

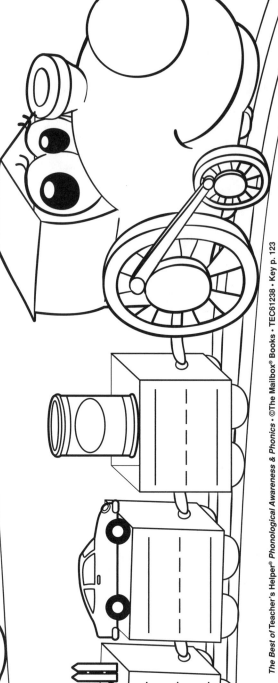

Name_____

Blimps Away!

✂ Cut. 🧴 Glue to match the beginning sounds.

✏ Write the beginning letter.

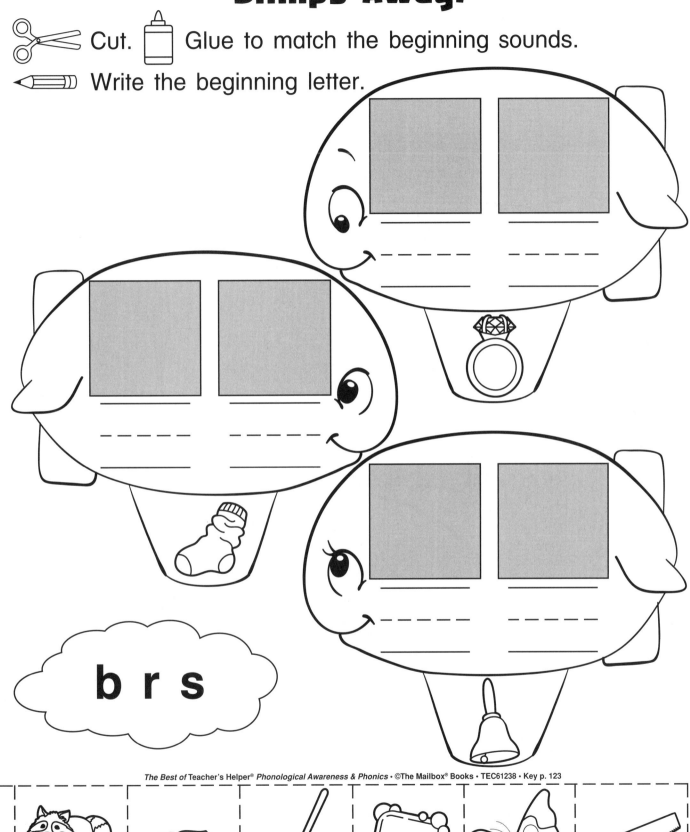

b r s

The Best of Teacher's Helper® *Phonological Awareness & Phonics* •©The Mailbox® Books • TEC61238 • Key p. 123

Name _____

Smooth Sailing

✂️ Cut. 🍾 Glue to match the beginning sounds.

✏️ Write the beginning letter.

l t z

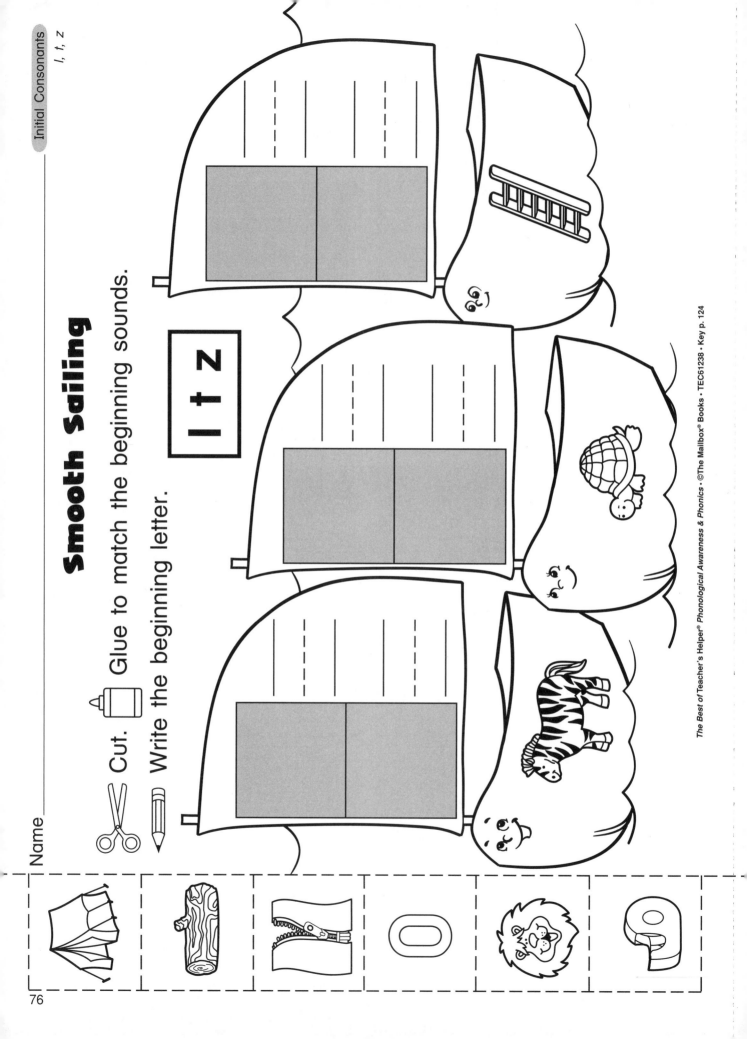

The Best of Teacher's Helper® Phonological Awareness & Phonics • ©The Mailbox® Books • TEC61238 • Key p. 124

Name_____

Blast Off!

✏️ Write the beginning letter.

🖍️ Color the matching star.

Name_____

Sky Sailing

Trace. ✏ Write.

✂ Cut. 🖊 Glue to match the ending sound.

Bb   Ll   Ss

The Best of Teacher's Helper® Phonological Awareness & Phonics • ©The Mailbox® Books • TEC61238 • Key p. 124

Name_____

Freefall Fun!

Trace. Write.

Cut. Glue to match the ending sound.

Ff   Gg   Rr

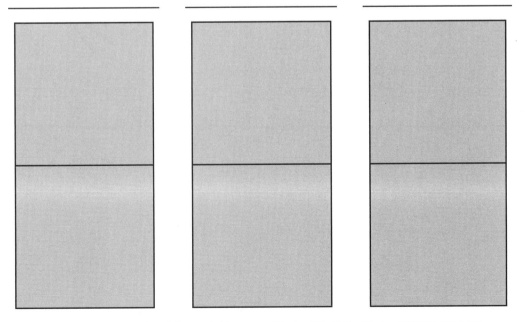

Name _____

Whee!

 Trace. 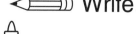 Write.

 Cut.  Glue to match the ending sound.

Dd   Kk   Nn

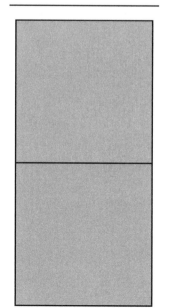

The Best of Teacher's Helper® Phonological Awareness & Phonics • ©The Mailbox® Books • TEC61238 • Key p. 124

Name _____

Treetop Landing

Trace.   Write.

Cut.   Glue to match the ending sound.

M m   P p   T t

Name_____

Drop Zone

 Write the letter of the ending sound.

 g

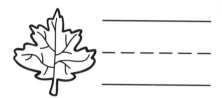

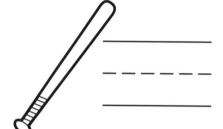

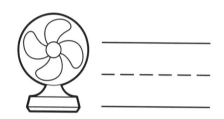

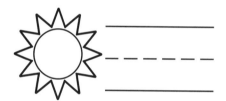

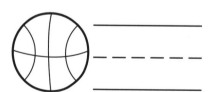

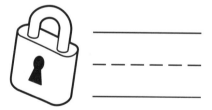

82

Plenty of Parachutes

Write the letter of the ending sound.

Name _____

A Tall Tail

 Trace the letter.

 Cut. Glue the ending sound.

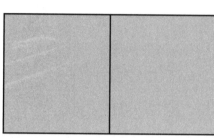
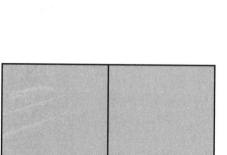
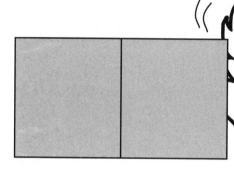

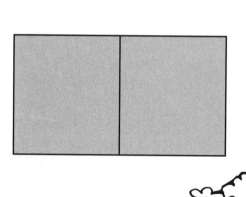
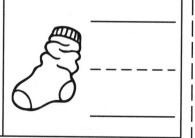

Write the ending letter.

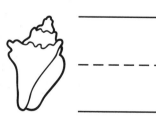

Name _____

Pretty Ponies

Final Consonants
b, f, r

Trace the letter.

Cut. Glue the ending sound.

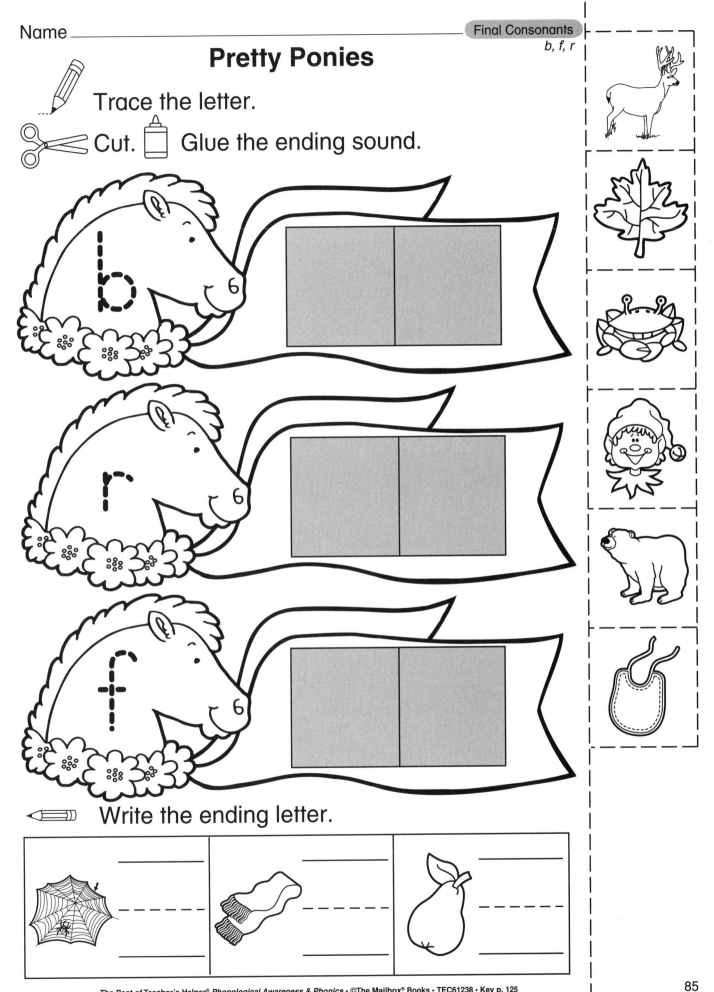

Write the ending letter.

The Best of Teacher's Helper® Phonological Awareness & Phonics • ©The Mailbox® Books • TEC61238 • Key p. 125

85

Butterfly Kiss

Trace the letter.

Cut. Glue the ending sound.

t

p

m

Write the ending letter.

___ ___

___ ___

___ ___

 The Best of Teacher's Helper® Phonological Awareness & Phonics • ©The Mailbox® Books • TEC61238 • Key p. 125

Name _____

Tailgate Party

Trace the letter.

Cut. Glue the ending sound.

d

s

g

Write the ending letter.

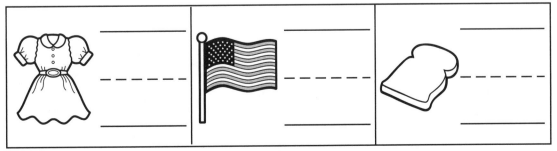

Name _____

Prairie Playtime

✏ Write the ending letter.

Name_____

Bubble Up!

Name each picture.

 Color by the code.

Color Code	
-ip —yellow	**-op** —blue

Name_____

Jump for Joy

 Cut.

 Glue under the correct word family.

 Write the word.

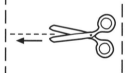

-un

-ut

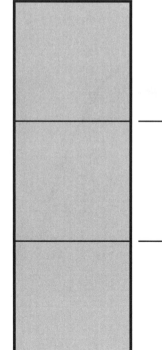 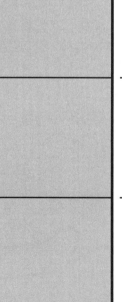

Twin Fins

 Circle each correct picture.

Write the word.

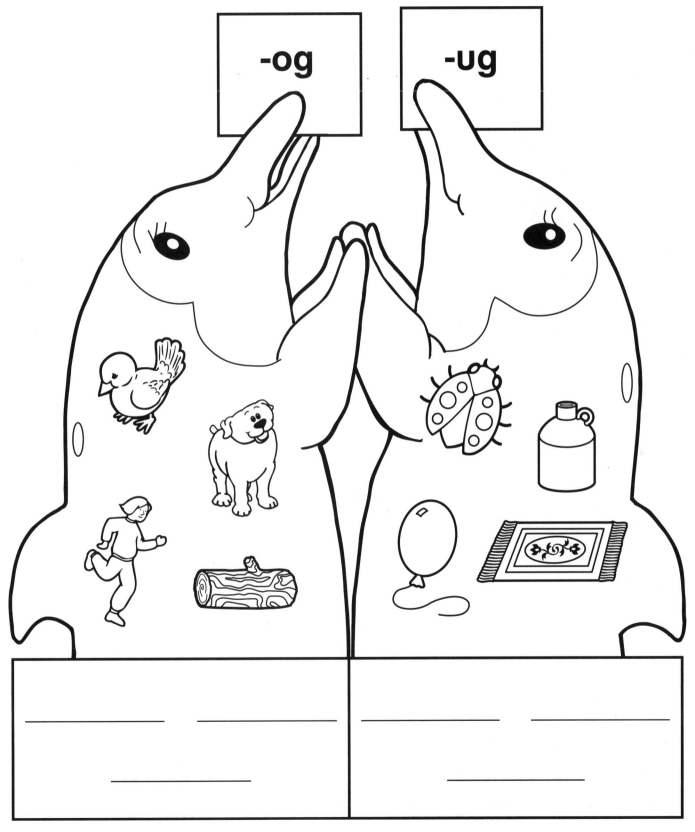

Flip-Flop

Name each picture.

Write the word.

Color.

The Best of Teacher's Helper® Phonological Awareness & Phonics • ©The Mailbox® Books • TEC61238 • Key p. 126

Chitter Chatter

Name each picture.

✏️ Draw a line to match the word.

🖍️ Color.

cap

map

nap

can

van

pan

Deep Diving

Read each word.

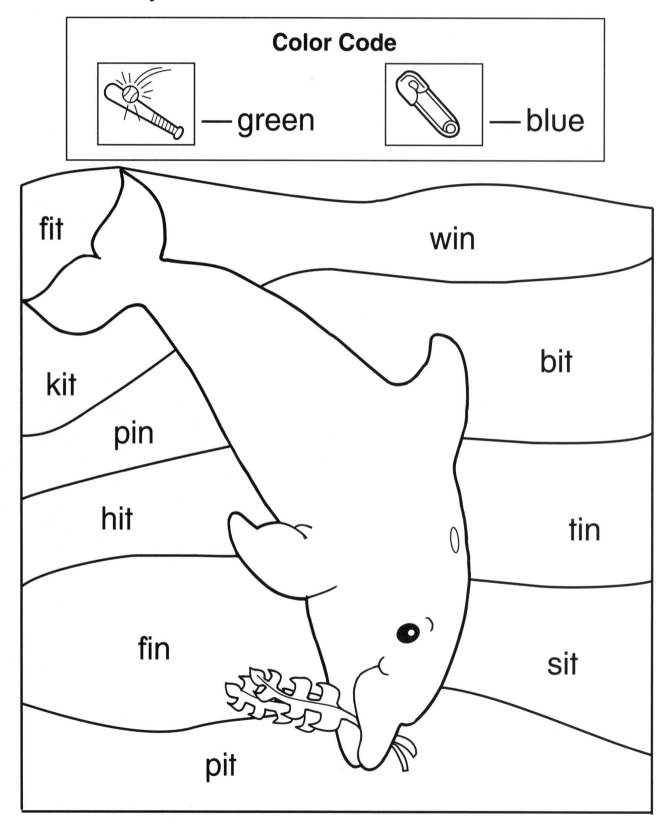

Color by the code.

Color Code

— green

— blue

fit

win

kit

bit

pin

hit

tin

fin

sit

pit

Name _____

Big Bug Race

✏ Write.

bug

The Best of Teacher's Helper® Phonological Awareness & Phonics • ©The Mailbox® Books • TEC61238 • Key p. 126

Name _____

Hanging Out

Circle the matching word family pictures.

Draw an X on the pictures that do not match.

The Best of Teacher's Helper® Phonological Awareness & Phonics • ©The Mailbox® Books • TEC61238 • Key p. 126

Little Helpers

○⟨▭▭ Circle the matching word family pictures.

⟨▭▭ Draw an X on the pictures that do not match.

-an

Drip-Dry

Circle the matching word family pictures.

Draw an X on the pictures that do not match.

The Best of Teacher's Helper® *Phonological Awareness & Phonics* • ©The Mailbox® Books • TEC61238 • Key p. 126

Name _____

Tall Tees

Circle the matching word family pictures.

Draw an X on the pictures that do not match.

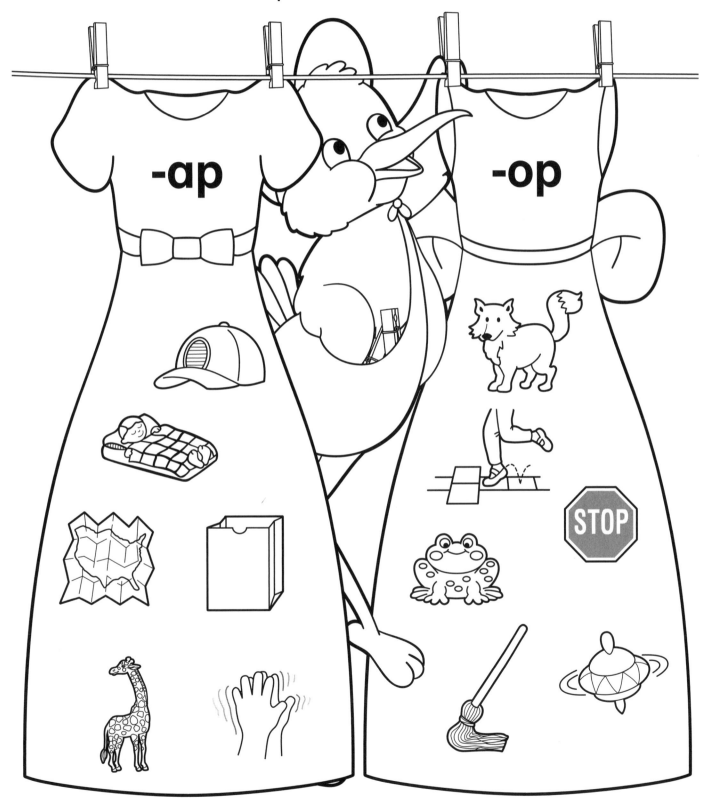

Summer Shirts

🖍 Color the matching word family pictures.

✏️ Write each word.

The Best of Teacher's Helper® *Phonological Awareness & Phonics* • ©The Mailbox® Books • TEC61238 • Key p. 127

Night Wash

Name each picture.

✏ Write each word.

-an	-at

pan

rat

_____

_____

_____

_____

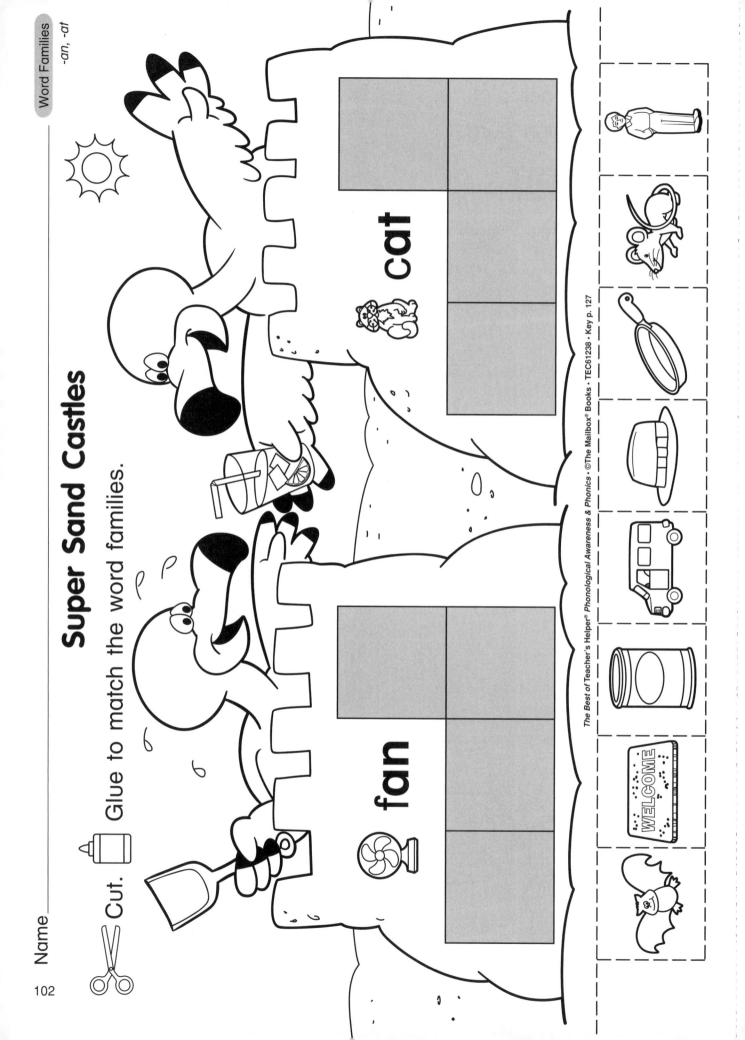

Super Sand Castles

✂ Cut. 🗌 Glue to match the word families.

cat

fan

Name _____

Refreshing Dreams

✂ Cut. 🖊 Glue to match the word families.

sock

mop

The Best of Teacher's Helper® Phonological Awareness & Phonics • ©The Mailbox® Books • TEC61238 • Key p. 127

103

Name _____

104

Lemonade, Please!

Write.

cat

sock

fan

mop

Name

Wading in Water

 Cut.

Glue to match the word families.

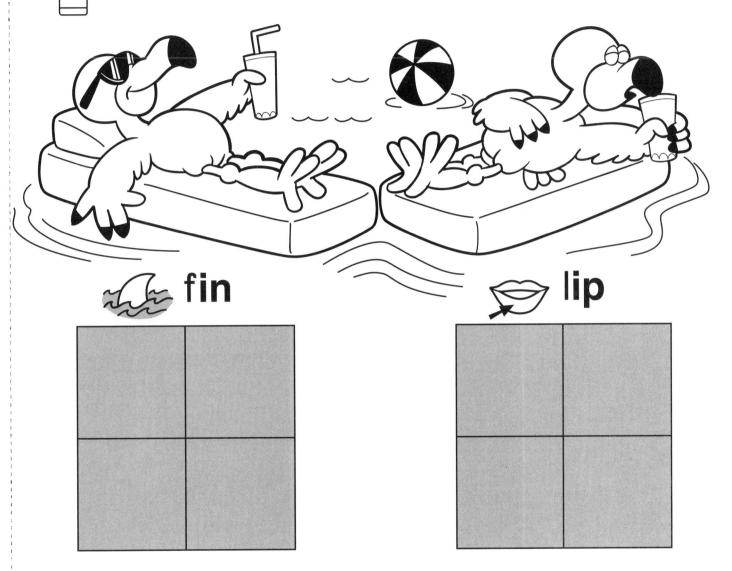

fin

lip

Name _____

106

Sipping in the Sun

✂ Cut. 🖊 Glue to match the word families.

nest

shell

Name _____

Making Homemade Lemonade!

Write.

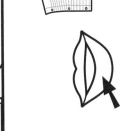 

lip

shell

fin

nest

Name_____

Flamingo Friends

Write.

 fan
_____

_ _ _ _ _ _ _ _ _ _ _ _
_____

 cat
_____

_ _ _ _ _ _ _ _ _ _ _ _
_____

 sock
_____

_ _ _ _ _ _ _ _ _ _ _ _
_____

 shell
_____

_ _ _ _ _ _ _ _ _ _ _ _
_____

 mop
_____

_ _ _ _ _ _ _ _ _ _ _ _
_____

 lip
_____

_ _ _ _ _ _ _ _ _ _ _ _
_____

fin
_____

_ _ _ _ _ _ _ _ _ _ _ _
_____

 nest
_____

_ _ _ _ _ _ _ _ _ _ _ _
_____

The Best of Teacher's Helper® *Phonological Awareness & Phonics* • ©The Mailbox® Books • TEC61238 • Key p. 128

Name _____

To the Top!

Trace.

Cut.

Glue to match.

fun	had
big	pop
jam	met

fun

pop

had

met

jam

big

The Best of Teacher's Helper® Phonological Awareness & Phonics • ©The Mailbox® Books • TEC61238 • Key p. 128

Name _____

No Peeking

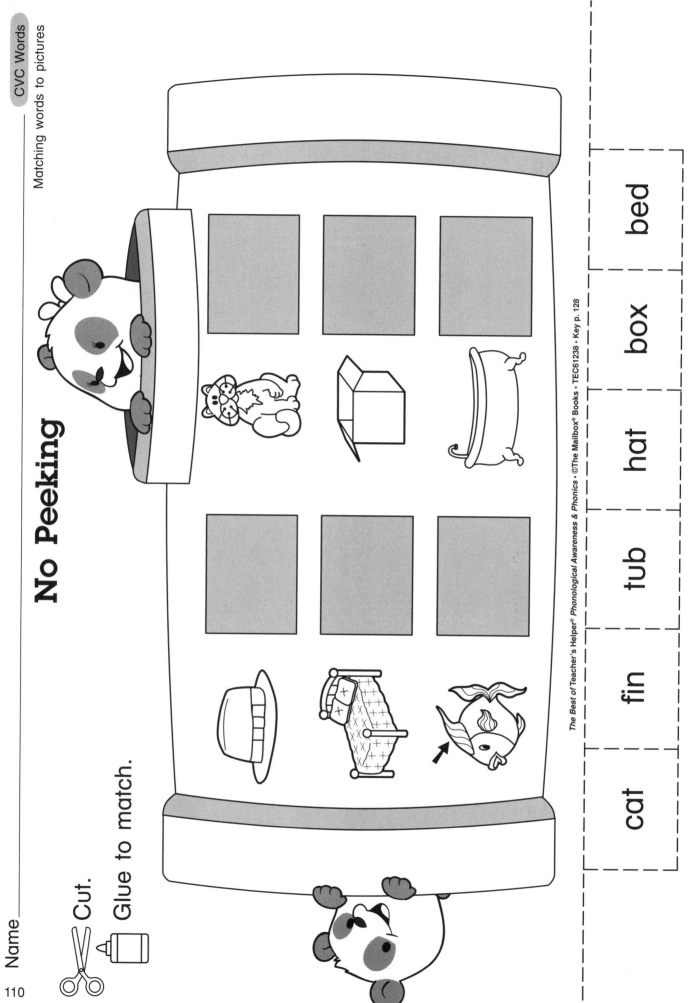

✂ Cut.

🧴 Glue to match.

cat	fin	tub	hat	box	bed

The Best of Teacher's Helper® Phonological Awareness & Phonics • ©The Mailbox® Books • TEC61238 • Key p. 128

Playing Around

Write the word for each picture.

Word Bank

| pig | can | sun |
| mop | web | bat |

Sandy Paws

Write the missing letter.

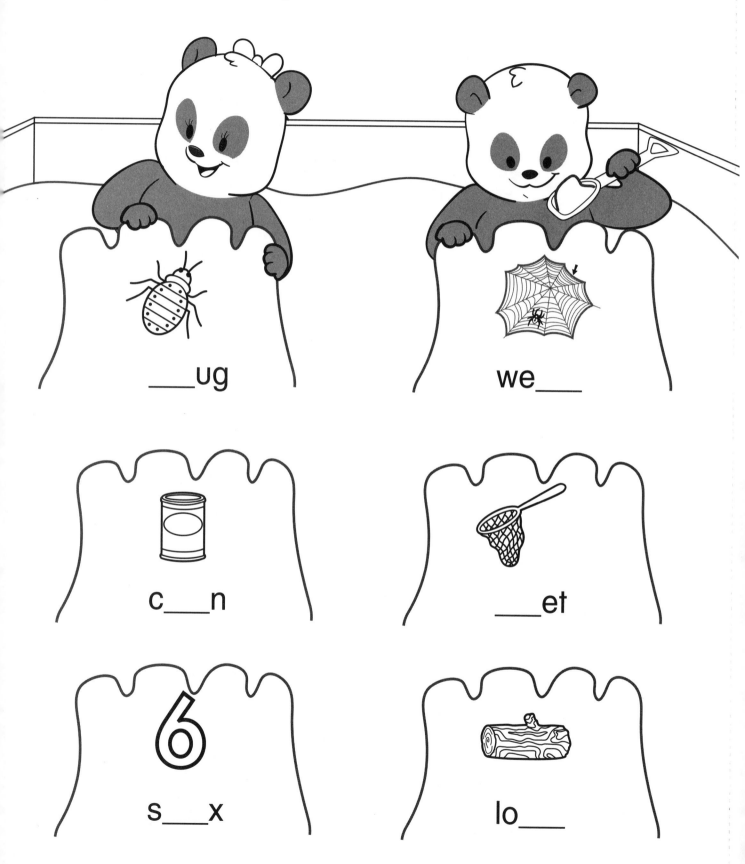

___ug

we___

c___n

___et

s___x

lo___

The Best of Teacher's Helper® Phonological Awareness & Phonics • ©The Mailbox® Books • TEC61238 • Key p. 128

Name

Hide-and-Seek

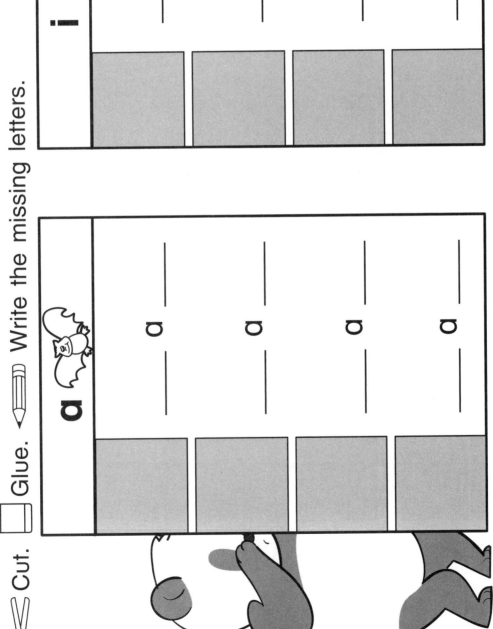

✂ Cut. Glue. ✏ Write the missing letters.

a

a _ _
a _ _
a _ _
a _ _

i

_ i _
_ i _
_ i _
_ i _

The Best of Teacher's Helper® Phonological Awareness & Phonics • ©The Mailbox® Books • TEC61238 • Key p. 128

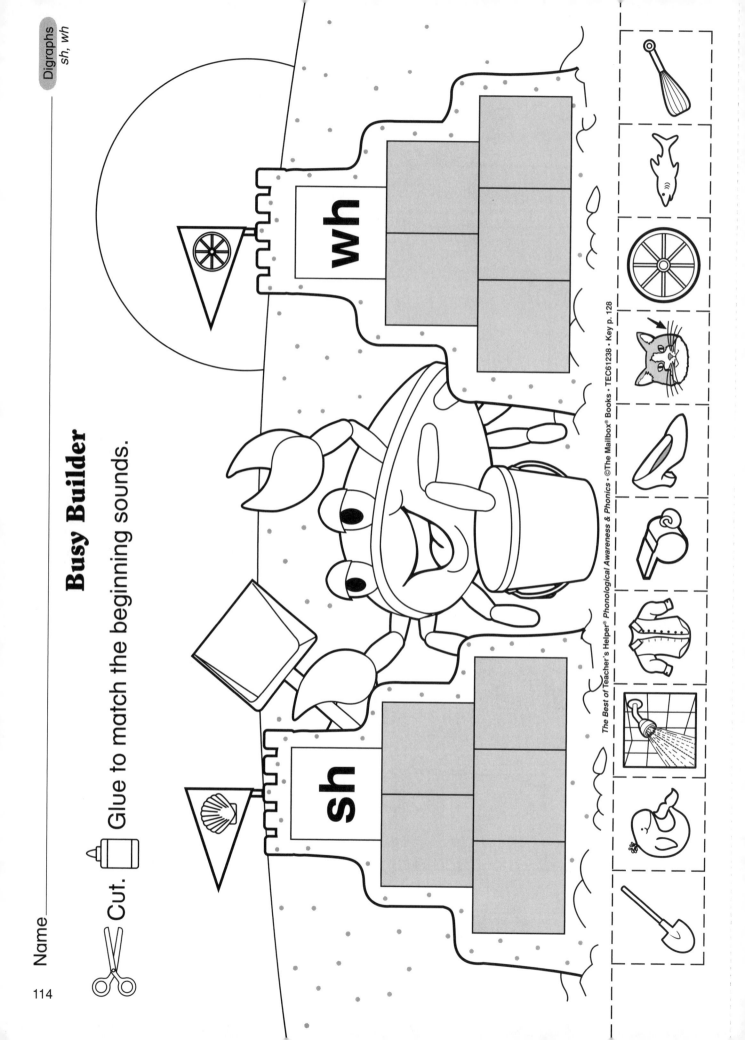

Busy Builder

Cut. Glue to match the beginning sounds.

sh

wh

The Best of Teacher's Helper® Phonological Awareness & Phonics • ©The Mailbox® Books • TEC61238 • Key p. 128

Answer Keys

Page 4

dog	**cat**
log	hat
jog	bat
frog	mat

Page 5

fox	**bear**
socks	chair
box	hair
blocks	pear

Page 6

hen	**goat**
ten	coat
pen	boat

Page 7

snake	**pig**
rake	wig
cake	dig

Page 8

bug	**bee**
mug	tree
rug	three
plug	key

Page 9

cake	**bun**
lake	sun
rake	run
snake	one

Page 10

bread	**jam**
head	ham
bed	lamb
thread	clam

Page 11

pear	**pie**
chair	eye
bear	tie
hair	cry

Page 12

corn	**chip**
horn	lip
thorn	rip
	zip

Page 13

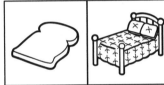
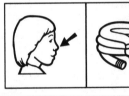

Page 14

Page 15

Page 16

Page 17

Page 18

mushroom
milk
macaroni
mug

Page 19

Order may vary.

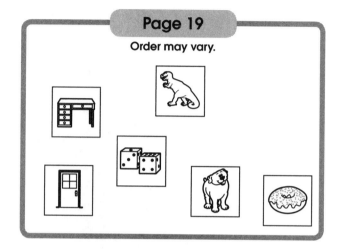

Page 20

Page 21

Order may vary.

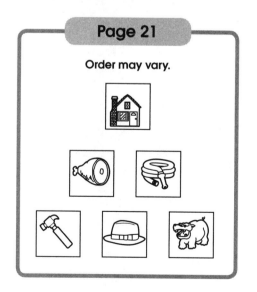

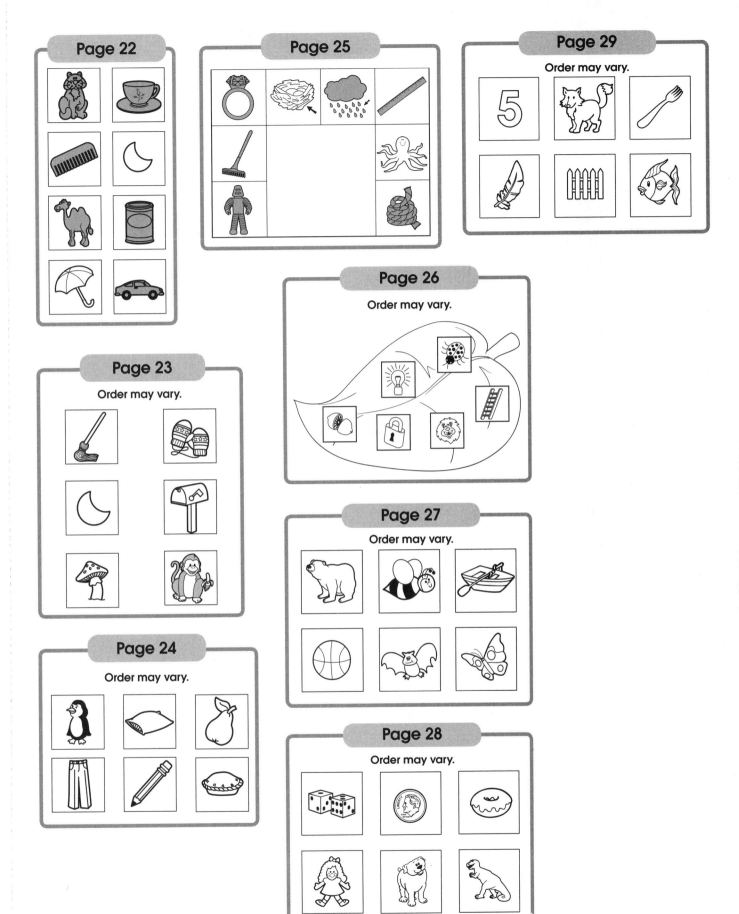

Page 30

Order may vary.

Page 31

Order may vary.

Page 32

Order may vary.

Page 33

Order may vary.

Page 34

Order may vary.

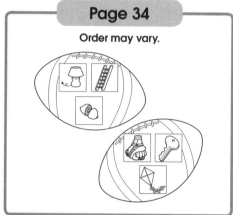

Page 35

Order may vary.

Page 36

Order may vary.

Order may vary.

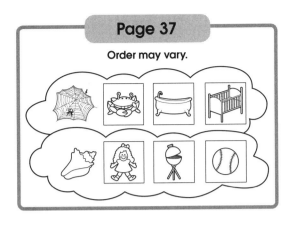

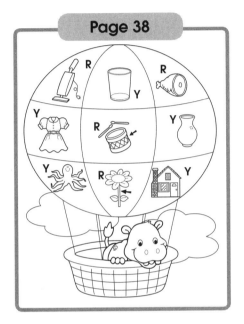

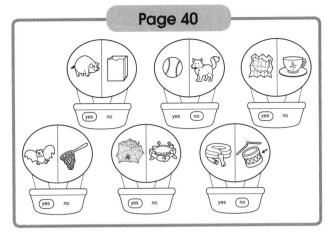

Order may vary.

Order may vary.

Order may vary.

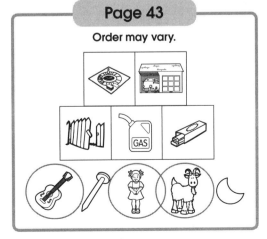

Page 44

Order may vary.

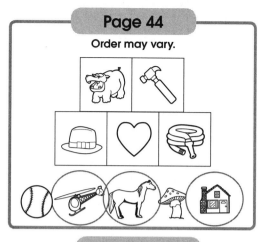

Page 45

Order may vary.

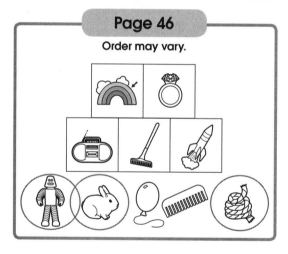

Page 46

Order may vary.

Page 47

Order may vary.

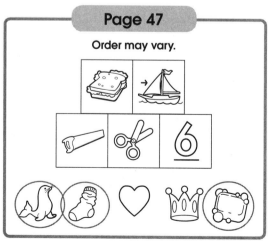

Page 48

Gate	Tickets
goat	telephone
girl	tape
game	turtle

Page 49

Order may vary.

Ball Throw	Ring Toss
book	rake
bird	rope
bike	ring

Page 50

Hot Dogs	Cotton Candy
heart	corn
hat	cake
house	cat

Page 51

Order may vary.

Dancer	Singer
deer	sun
dog	saw
doughnut	sock
duck	soap

Page 52

Jam	Pies
jeep	pants
jump rope	pencil
jelly beans	paint
jar	pizza

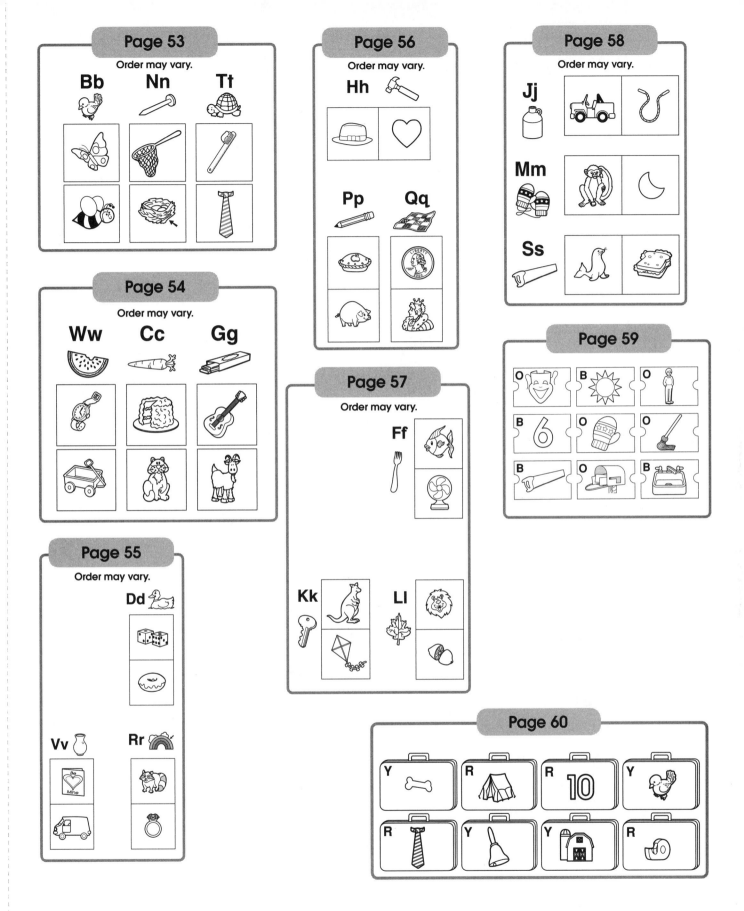

Page 61

Order may vary.

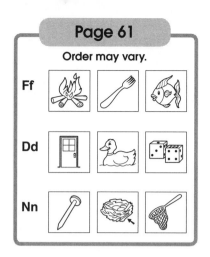

Ff
Dd
Nn

Page 62

Order may vary.

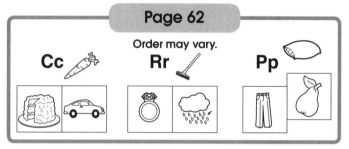

Cc   Rr   Pp

Page 63

Order may vary.

Hh   Gg   Ll

Page 64

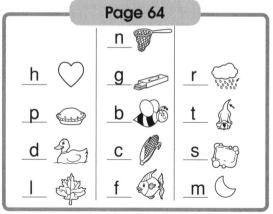

h   n
p   g   r
d   b   t
l   c   s
       f   m

Page 65

Page 66

Order may vary.

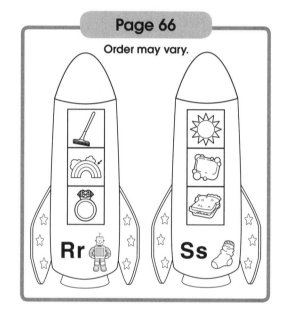

Rr   Ss

Page 67

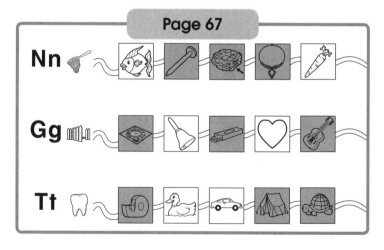

Nn

Gg

Tt

Page 68

Order may vary.

Cc **Jj** **Pp**

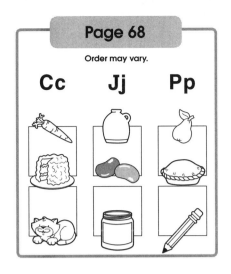

Page 69

Page 70

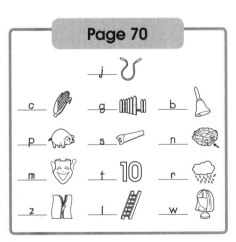

Page 71

Order may vary.

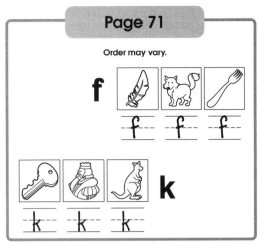

Page 72

Page 73

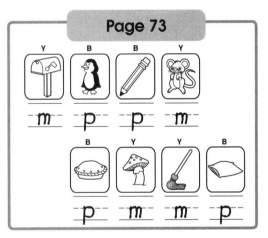

Page 74

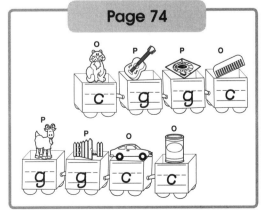

Page 75

Order may vary.

Page 76

Order may vary.

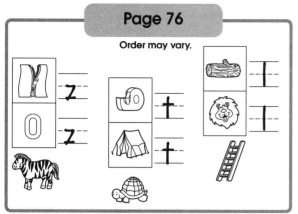

Page 77

Page 78

Order may vary.

Bb	**Ll**	**Ss**
Bb	Ll	Ss

Page 79

Order may vary.

Ff	**Gg**	**Rr**
Ff	Gg	Rr

Page 80

Order may vary.

Dd	**Kk**	**Nn**
Dd	Kk	Nn

Page 81

Order may vary.

Mm	**Pp**	**Tt**
Mm	Pp	Tt

Page 82

g	f
t	n
k	n
t	k
t	g

Page 83

The Best of Teacher's Helper® Phonological Awareness & Phonics • ©The Mailbox® Books • TEC61238

Page 84

Order may vary.

l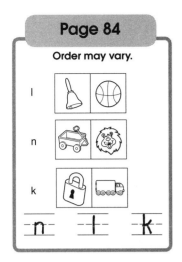

n

k

n   t   k

Page 85

Order may vary.

b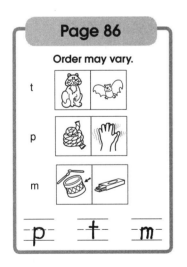

r

f

b   f   r

Page 86

Order may vary.

t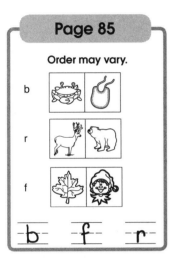

p

m

p   t   m

Page 87

Order may vary.

d

s

g

s   g   d

Page 88

k   p   t

n   m   t

b   g

n

Page 89

Page 90

Order may vary.

-un		-ut	
	bun		nut
	run		hut
	sun		cut

Page 91

Order may vary.

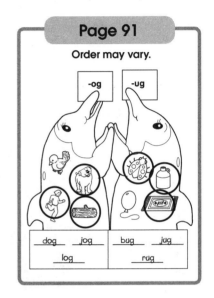

-og		-ug	
dog	jog	bug	jug
log		rug	

Page 92

-ot   cot   dot
              pot

-at   rat   bat
       hat   cat

Page 93

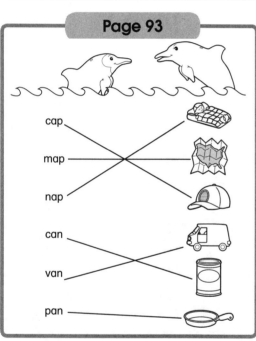

cap
map
nap

can
van

pan

Page 94

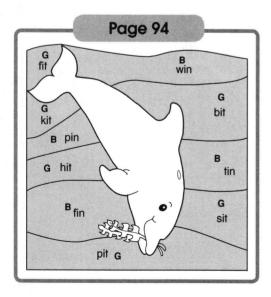

G fit   B win
G kit   G bit
B pin
G hit   B tin
B fin   G sit
pit G

Page 95

bug
mug
rug

jug
hug

Page 96

-at

Page 97

-an

Page 98

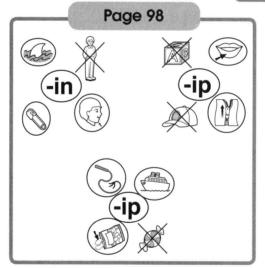

-in   -ip

-ip

Page 99

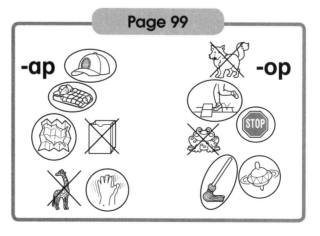

-ap   -op

Page 100

Order may vary.

-ap

cap

map

nap

-op

top

mop

hop

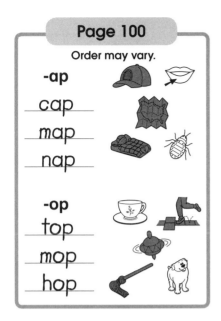

Page 101

-an		**-at**	
pan	fan	rat	mat
man	can	bat	hat
	van	cat	

Page 102

Order may vary.

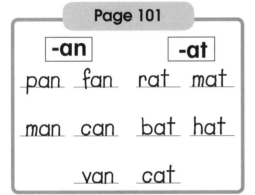 fan

cat

Page 103

Order may vary.

mop

s**ock**

Page 104

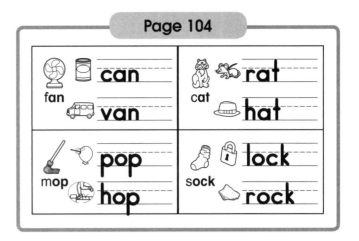

fan — **can**

— **van**

cat — **rat**

— **hat**

mop — **pop**

— **hop**

sock — **lock**

— **rock**

Page 105

Order may vary.

fin

lip

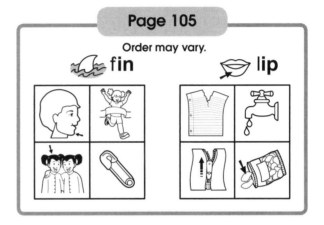

Page 106

Order may vary.

sh**ell**

nest

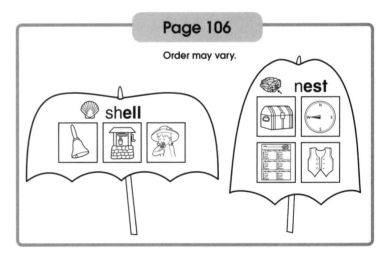

Page 107

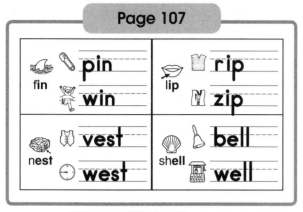

fin — **pin**	lip — **rip**
— **win**	— **zip**
nest — **vest**	shell — **bell**
— **west**	— **well**

Page 108

fan — **can**	cat — **bat**
sock — **rock**	shell — **bell**
mop — **hop**	lip — **rip**
fin — **win**	nest — **test**

Page 109

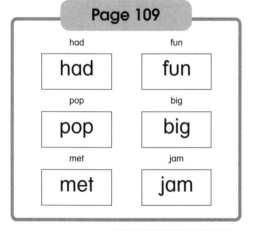

had — had	fun — fun
pop — pop	big — big
met — met	jam — jam

Page 110

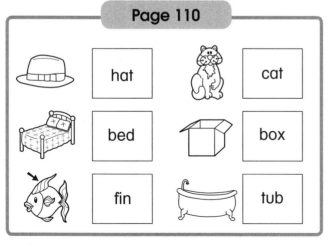

hat   cat

bed   box

fin   tub

Page 111

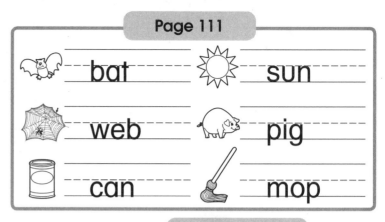

— bat	— sun
— web	— pig
— can	— mop

Page 112

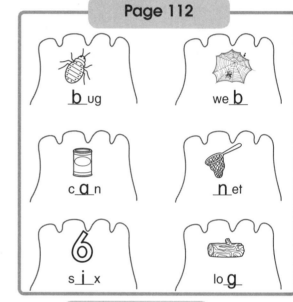

b_ug   we b

c a n   _n et

s i x   lo g

Page 113

Order may vary.

a	i
f a n	w i g
b a g	d i g
h a t	l i p
m a p	b i b

Page 114

Order may vary.

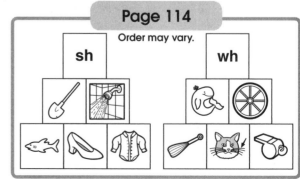

| sh | wh |

128